LET'S MAKE A SPECIAL RING

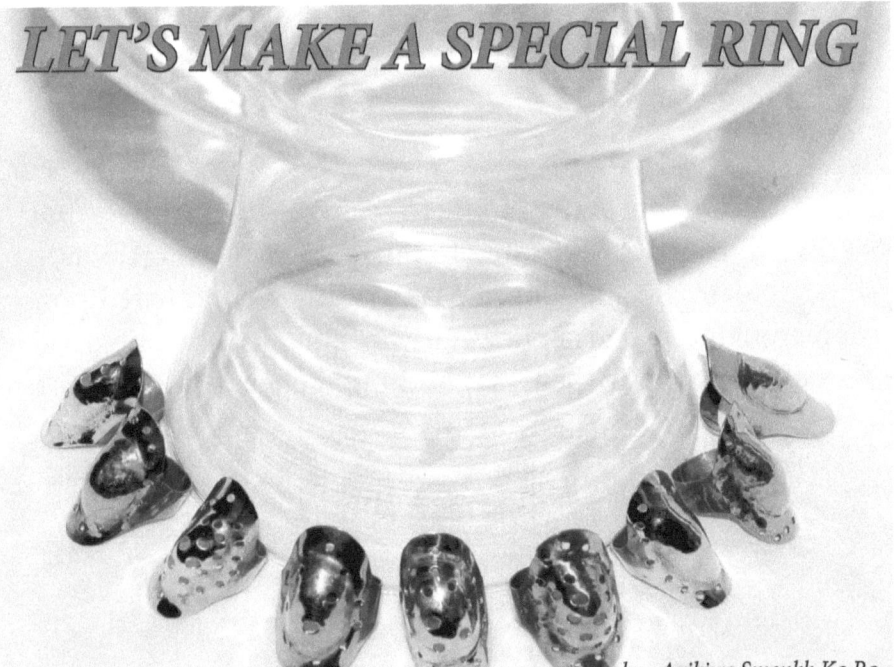

by Azikiwe Smenkh Ka Ra

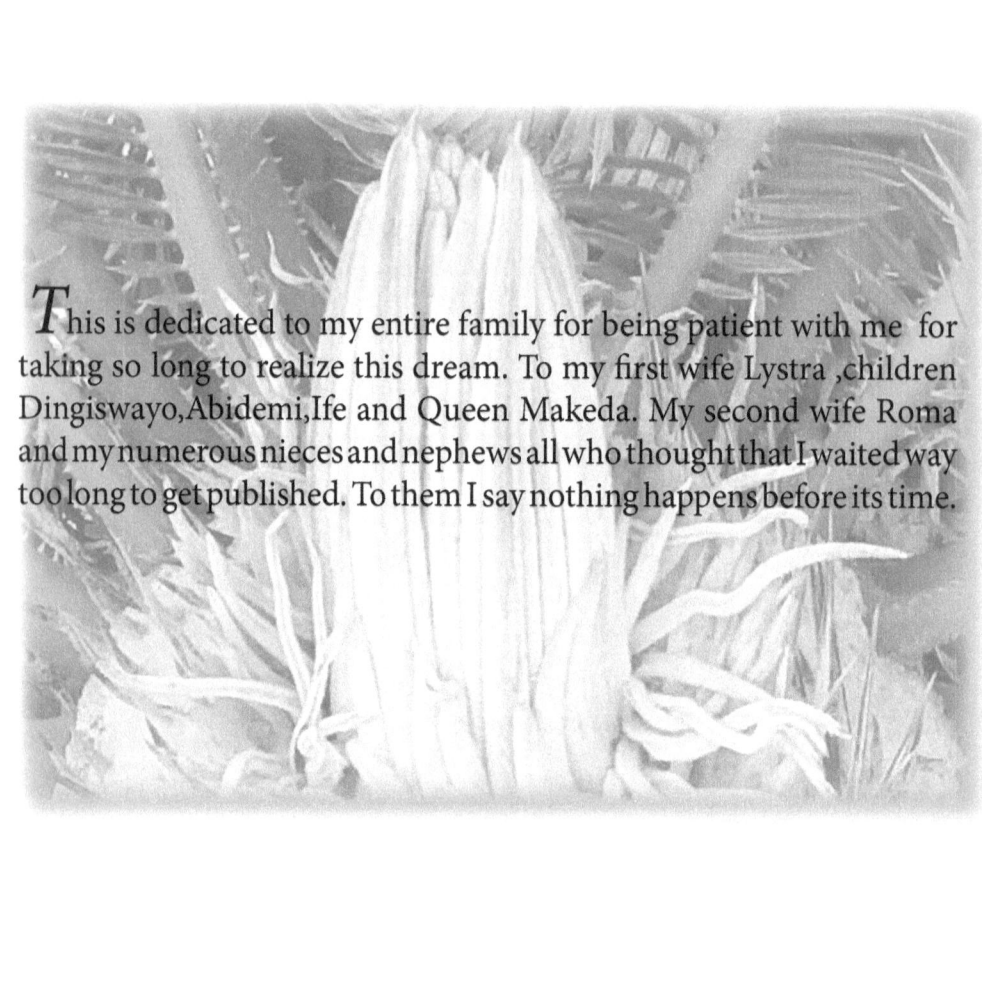

This is dedicated to my entire family for being patient with me for taking so long to realize this dream. To my first wife Lystra ,children Dingiswayo,Abidemi,Ife and Queen Makeda. My second wife Roma and my numerous nieces and nephews all who thought that I waited way too long to get published. To them I say nothing happens before its time.

As we started this tutorial one of the projects that we said we would do a tutorial for was the making of one of these rings. I know that I am a long way from keeping my promise but I am keeping it all the same.

TOOLS NEEDED

The tools we would need would be some of the following ;
a jeweler's saw like the one shown below

with a no.0 or a no.1 blade a ballpein hammer(one side flat and the other round) this I got at a discount store for about $2.00 ,a sheet of 20g of copper ,a torch for annealing the metal and soldering the joints,drill and drill bits for drilling the holes,

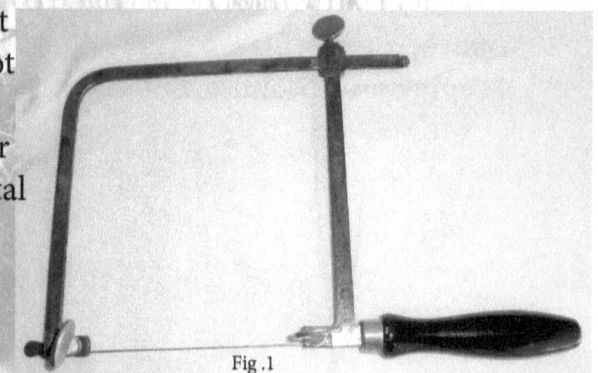

Fig .1

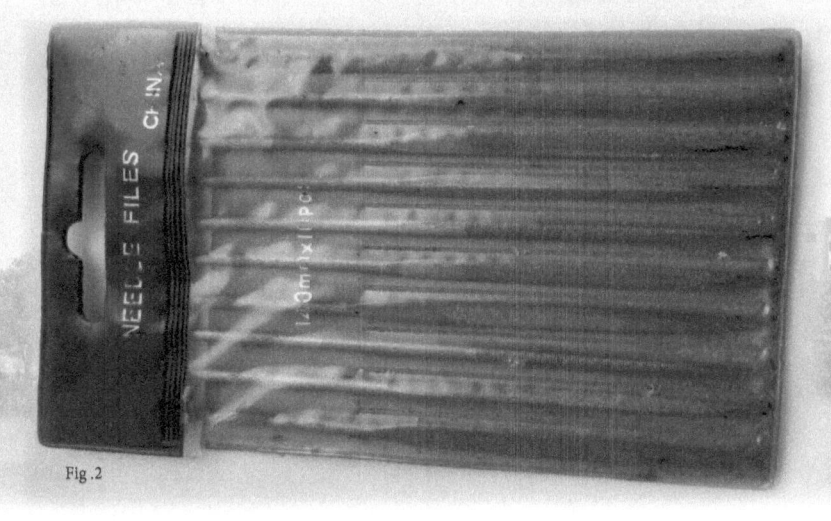

Fig .2

a file for smoothing the edges, or better still if you can put your hands on a set of needle files , a polishing wheel , a bench grinder like the one I am using in one of the pictures ,or you can use the drill with a polishing pad attachment,
 a doming block or as I did ,use a block of wood to create an indentation that would give you the shape of the dome in the finished piece. In this tutorial I used a metal ring that I found

Fig.3

These are some of the tools you will need if you intend to get into jewelry making as a hobby or to follow your passion.
I make a point of seeking out the most inexpensive tools I can find and I even make some of my own .

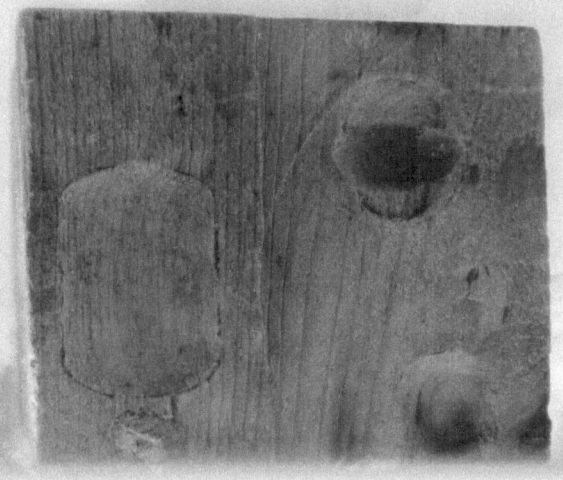

Fig.4

I made the copper thongs pictured here.

I use this to retrieve my annealed and soldered pieces from the cleaning solution. No need to spend a whole lot of money. This was made from one length of copper wire about eighteen inches long .

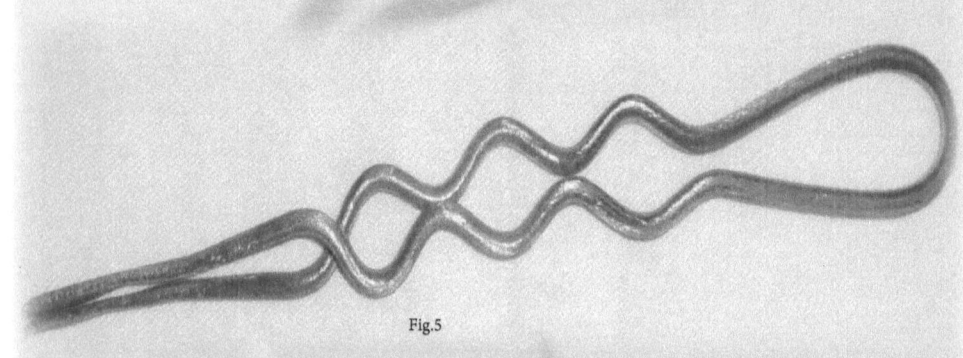

Fig.5

Pictured here is my faithful hand torch .now it can be uncomfortable but after much use you become fairly competent . You can make many beautiful pieces with this torch ,and it is cheap . My favorite word.

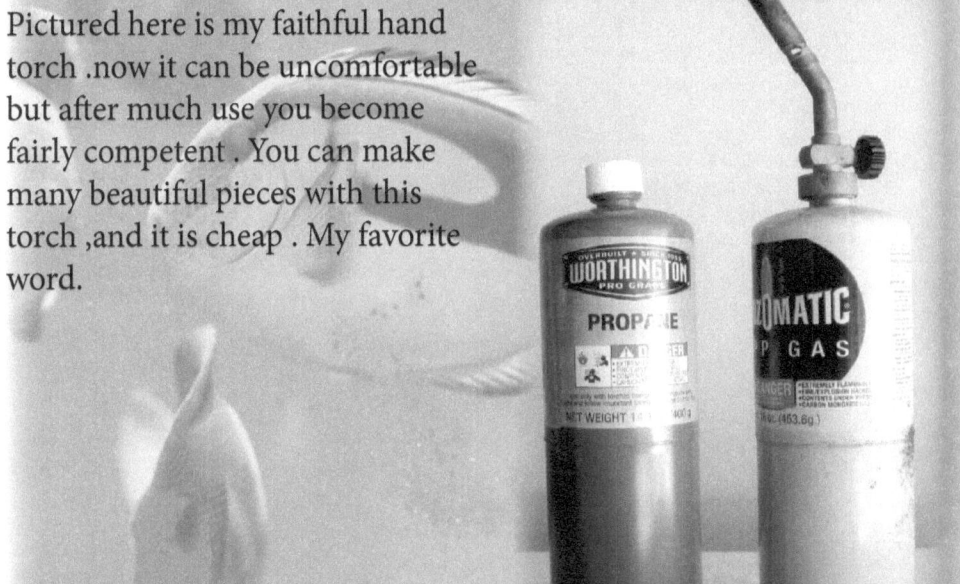

Fig.6

Ball pein hammer and shoemaker awl for making indentations
and holes when necessary.

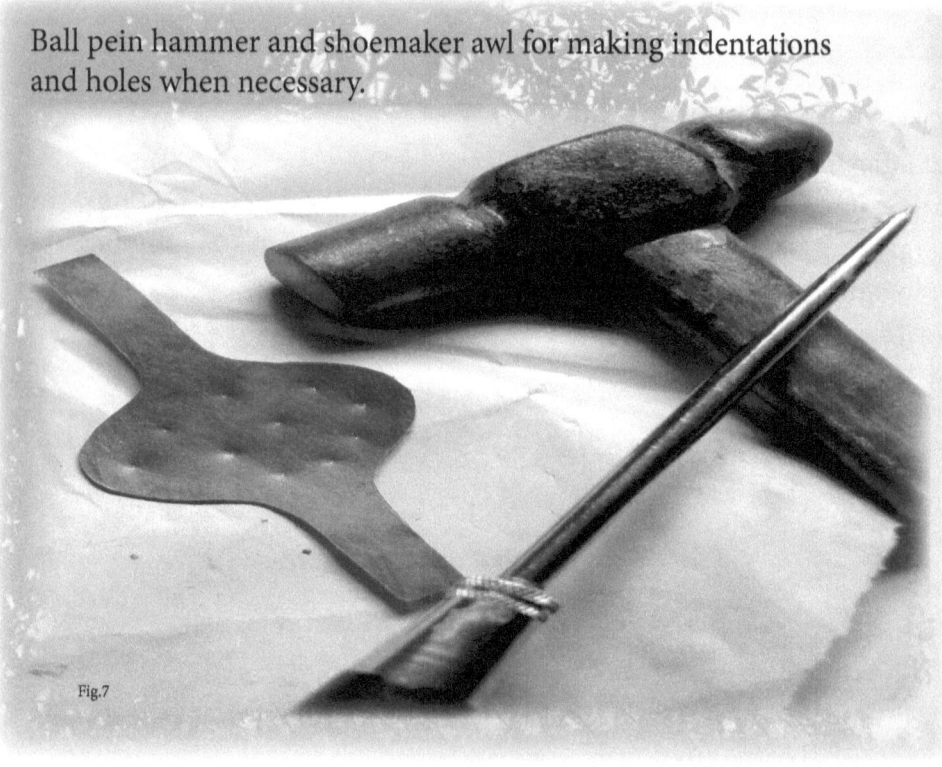

Fig.7

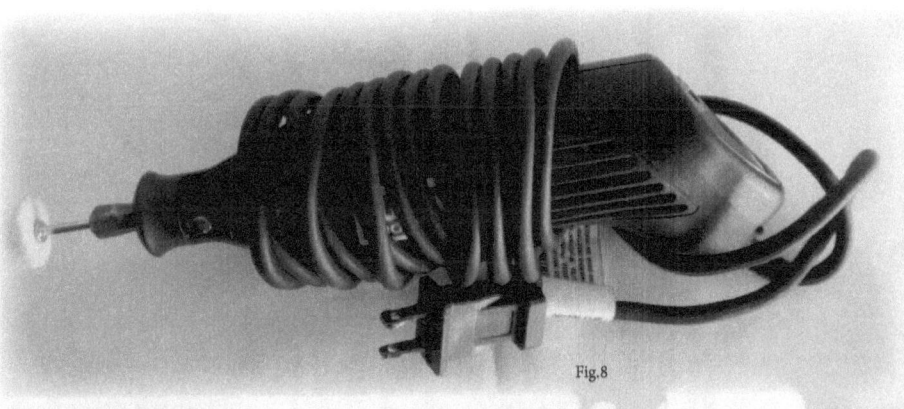

Fig.8

This example of a buffering wheel (pictured below) can be used along with a normal hand drill (pictured above).

Buffering wheel

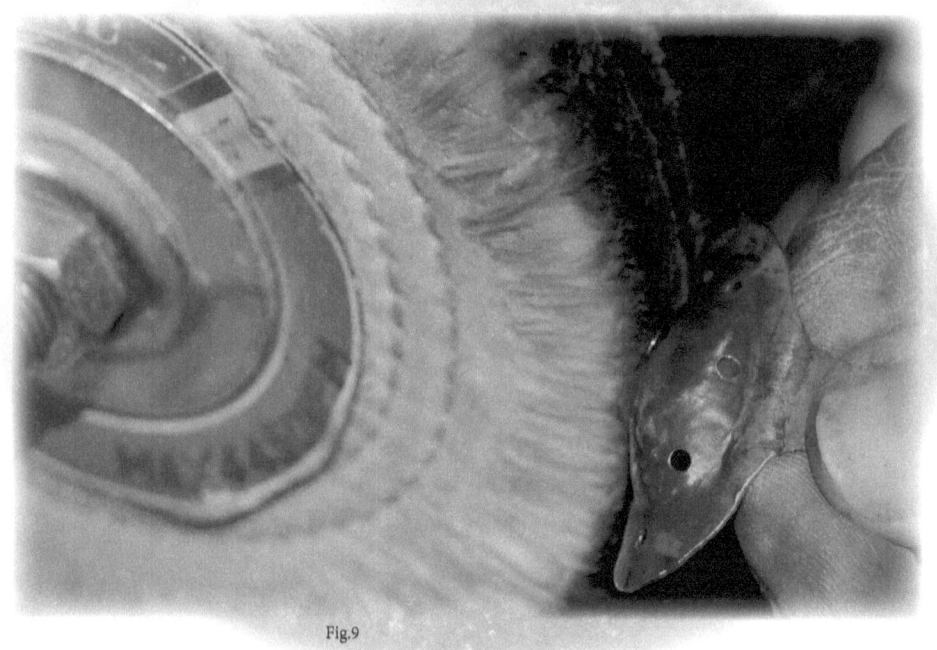

Fig.9

THE PROCESS

You will need a pattern in this shape . This is going to be the beginning of your ring.   After laying out and drawing your pattern on the metal you are going start cutting with your saw . The fun is about to begin .

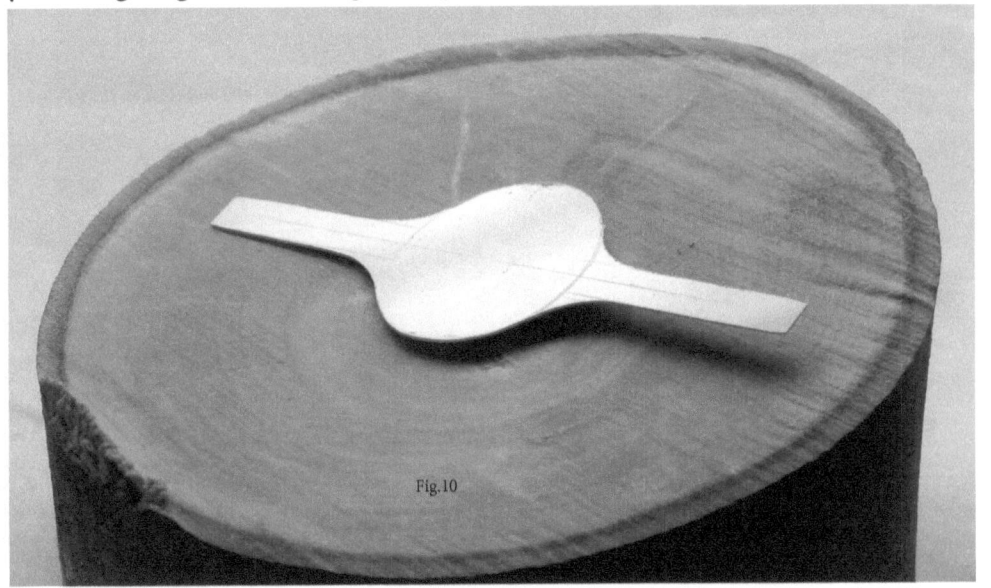

Fig.10

Let me be quick to point that the angle at which I am holding the saw is not the correct one . It is better when the saw is at a 90 degree angle , but after a number of years I have grown accustomed to different angles and they work for me. I was also the photographer for this entire tutorial .

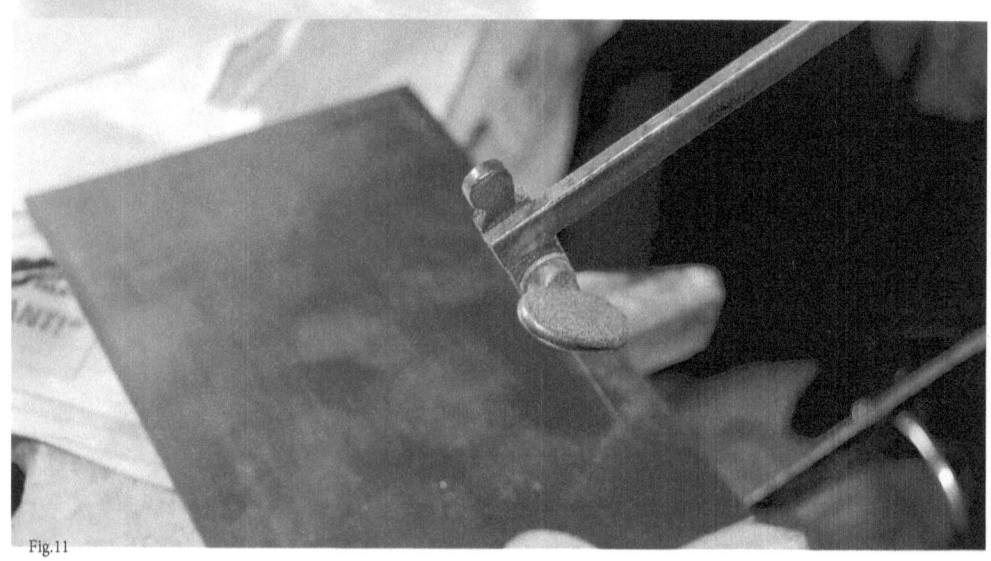

Fig.11

Do not follow me and get greedy . After cutting this is what you end up with . When I am in production mode I tend to do several pieces at one time . If you are in the mood then by all means go for it.

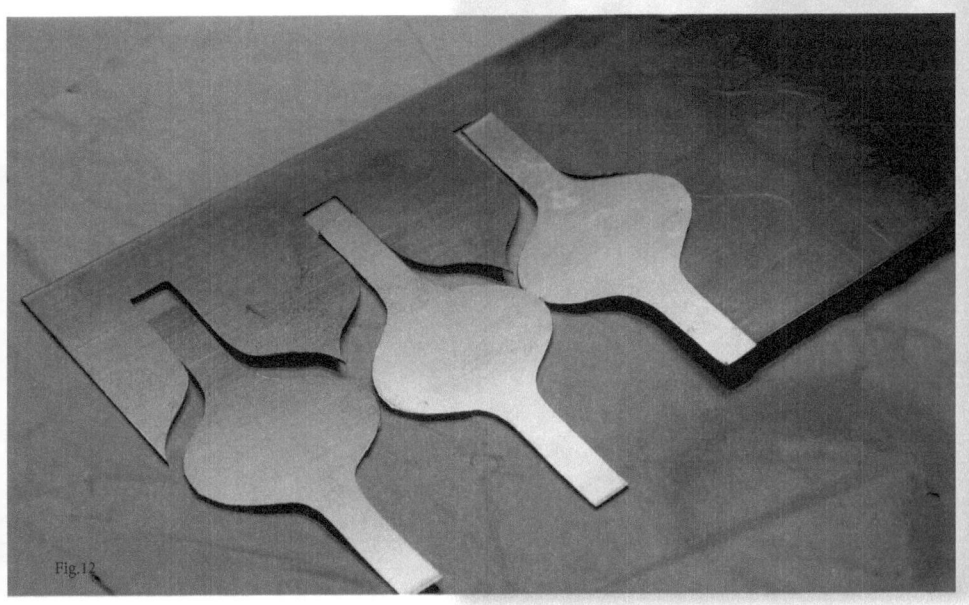

Fig.12

I now take my ball pein hammer and shoemaker awl and begin to make small indentations in the metal ,these are actual starter points for me to drill the design holes .

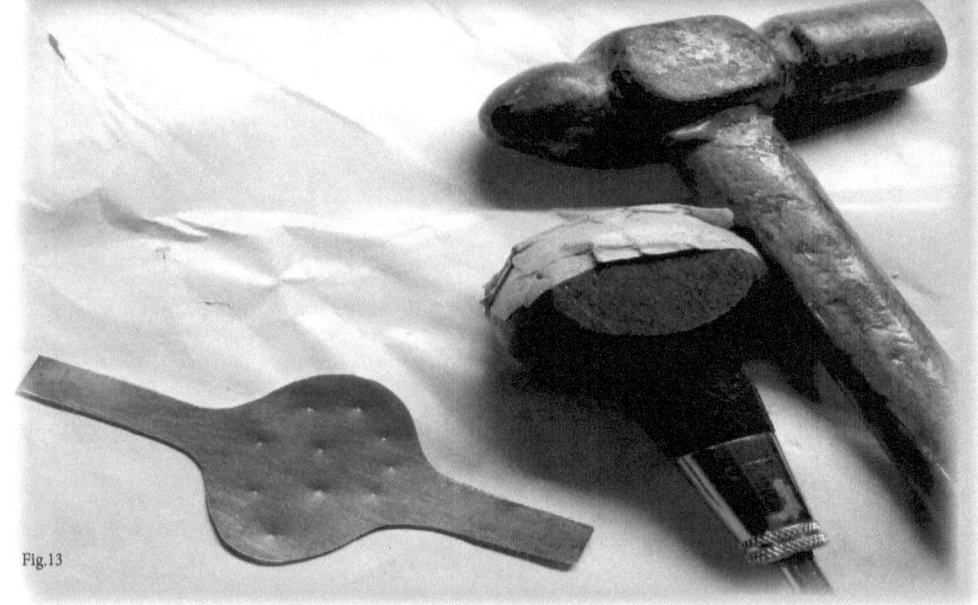

Fig.13

The holes have been drilled.

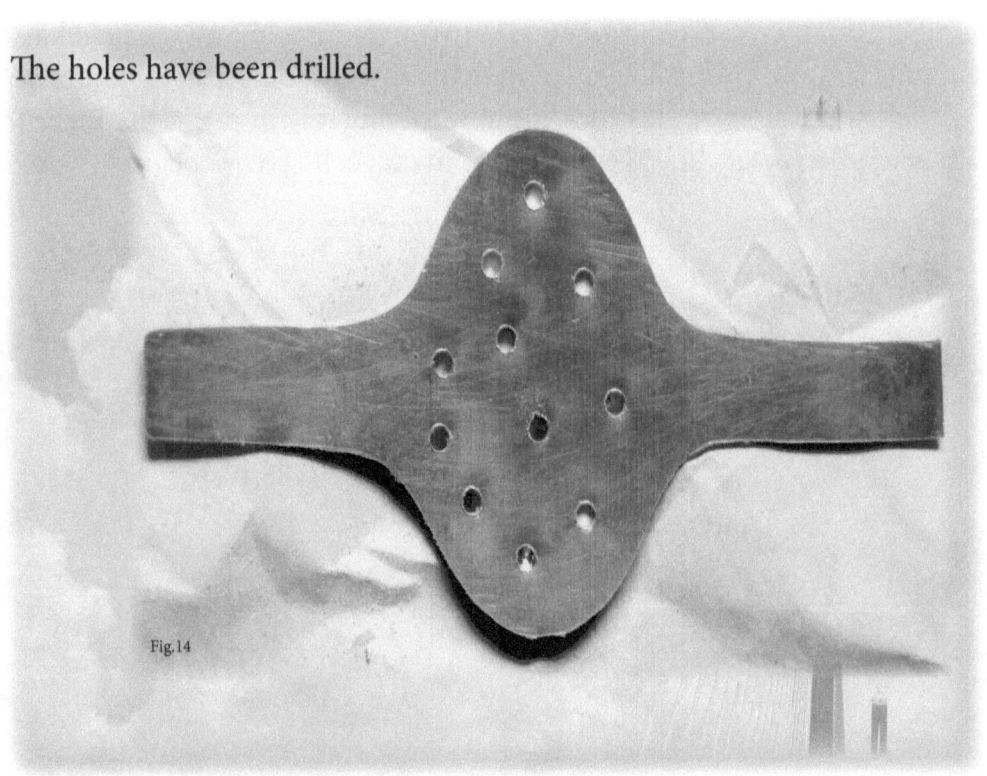

Fig.14

Some tutorials would recommend that you go out and buy special charcoal blocks to do your soldering and firing ,but as you see I went outside and picked up an extra clay block that was lying idle in the yard . Recycle . Recycle . On blocks like these some of my favorite pieces begin to take shape.

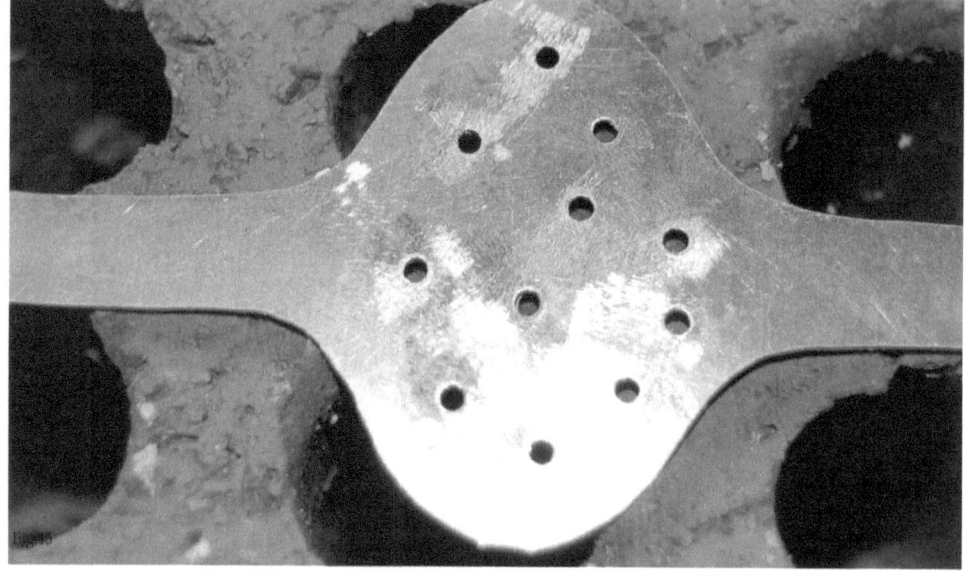

the tie-dye effect that you see on the metal . We refer to
that as fire scale and it would be taken care of later . But
first we

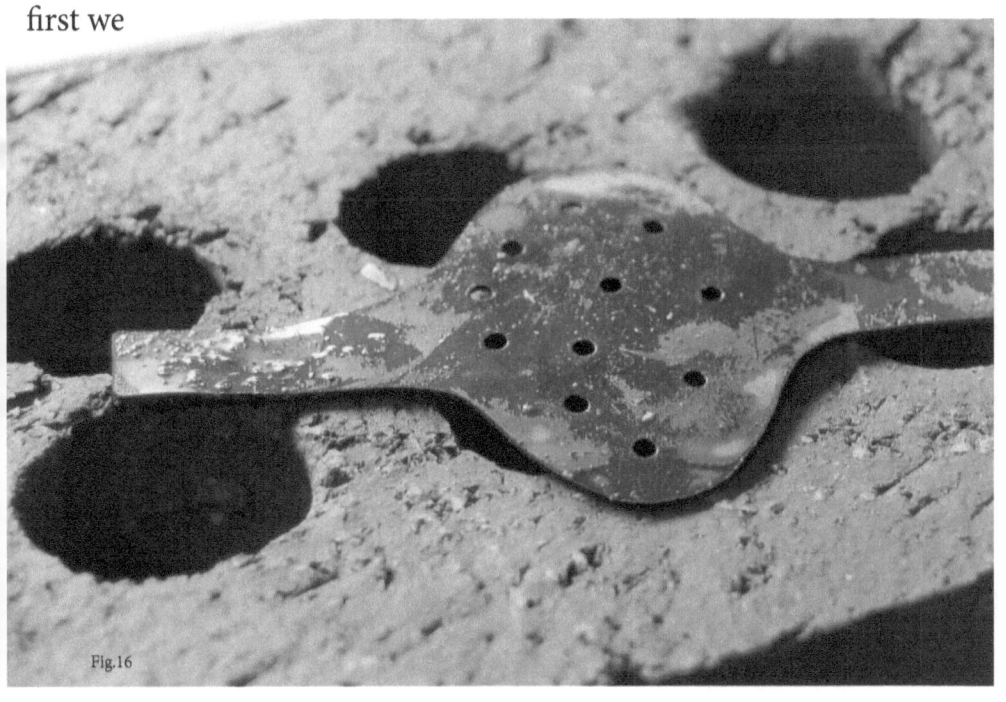

Fig.16

I put fire to the metal until.............

it begins to glow red ,this the ideal stage for what is to come next. This stage is called annealing ,it is the softening of the metal which would make it easier to work with.

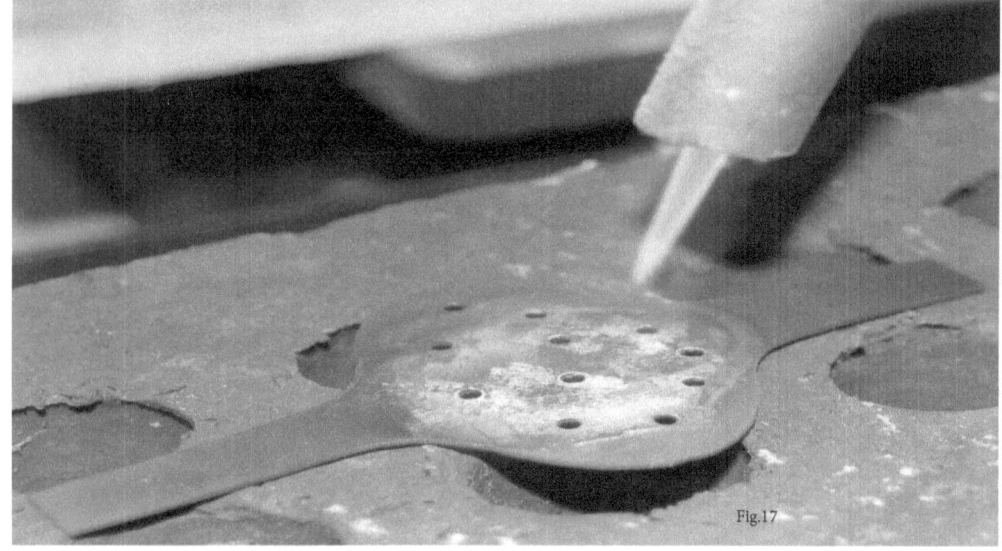

Fig.17

Cool the hot metal . I am not touching that hot metal.

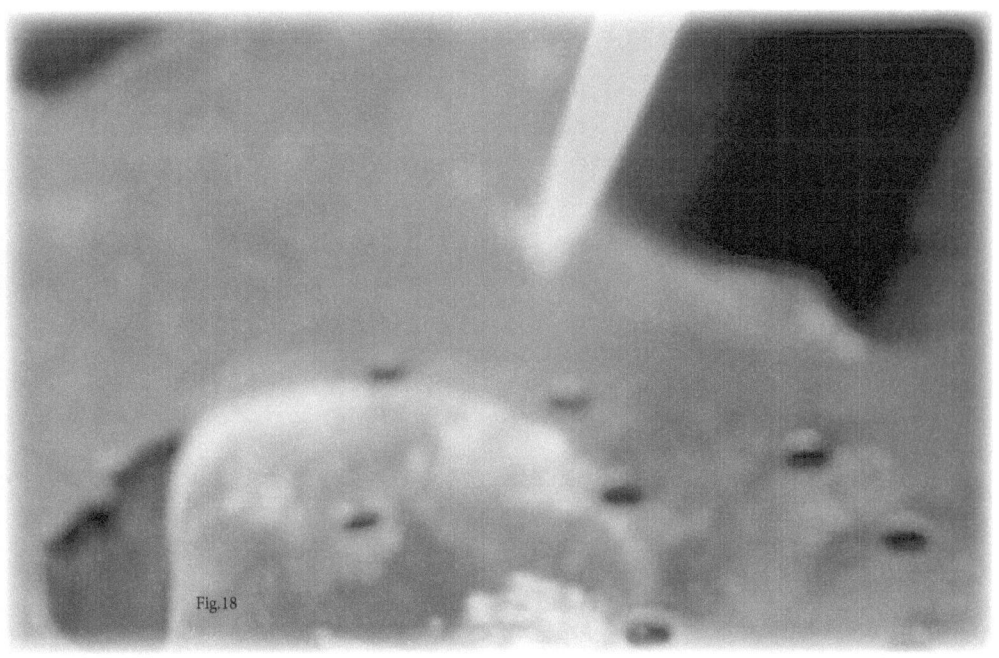

Fig.18

I take my pliers or thong (home made of course) and carefully pick it up and place it in the bowl of cold water . Then ....

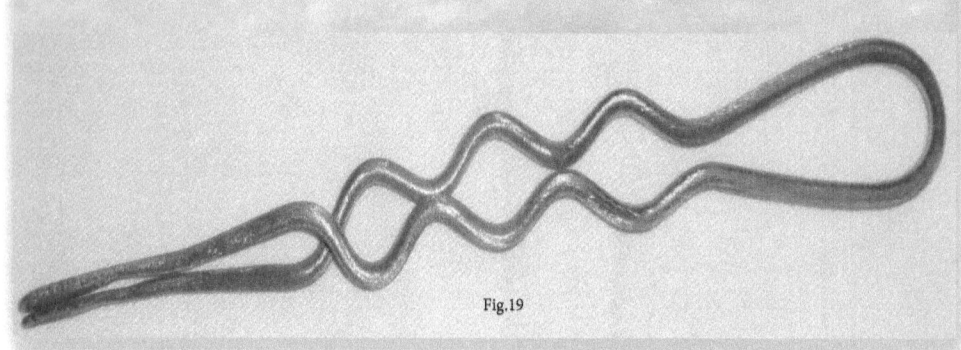

Fig.19

Time to shine . We now have to clean off the rest of the fire scale that might have been too stubborn to come loose in the pickle. Time to shine some more. And some more.

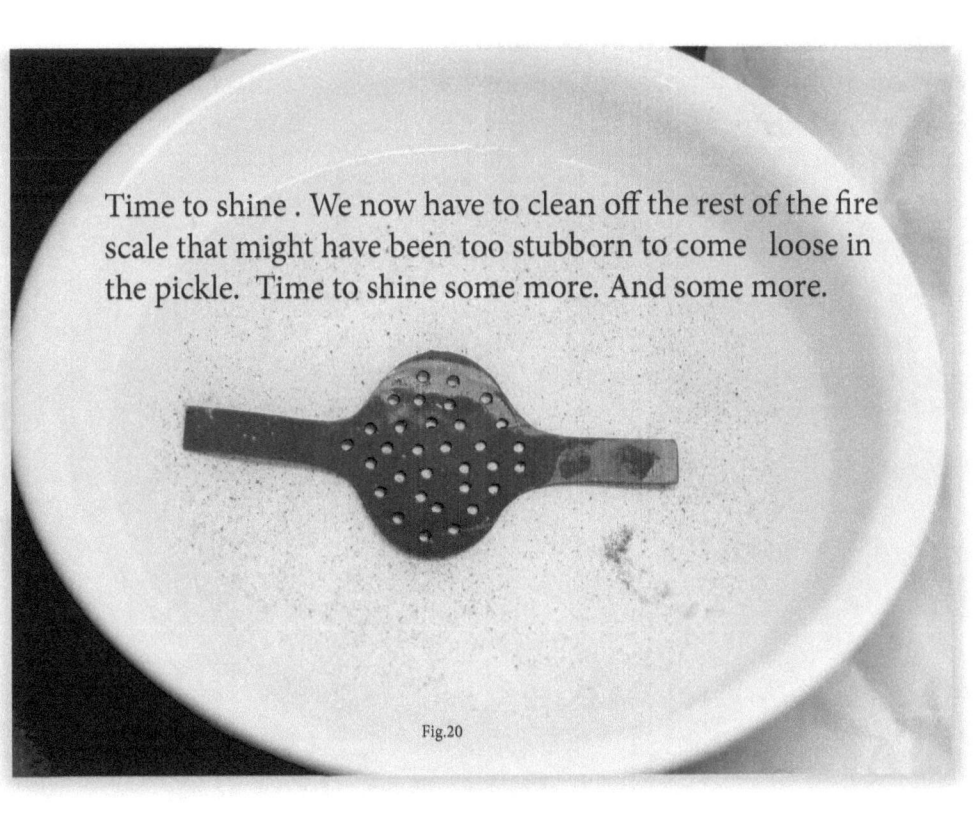

Fig.20

we bring this little found object into play. I found this as I was walking along the street looking for money that someone might have thrown away .

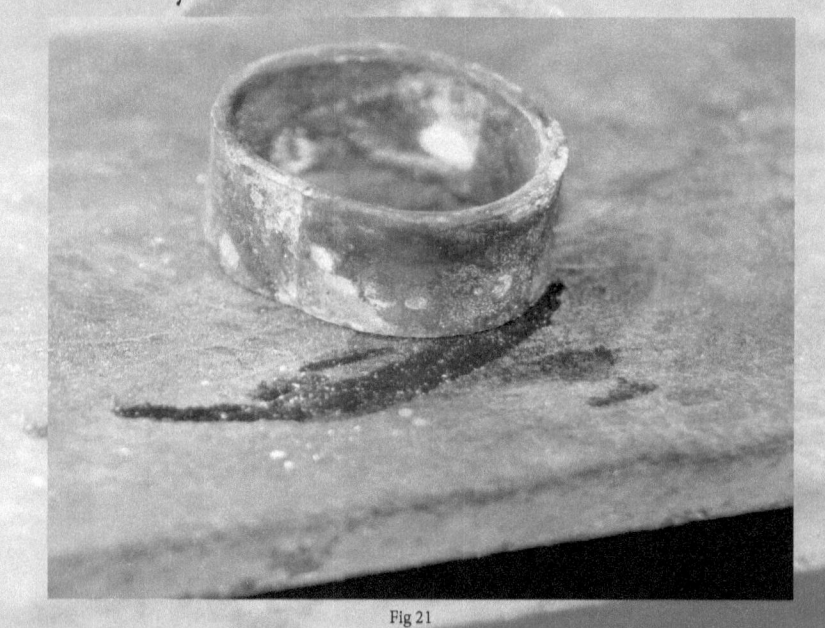

Fig 21

Everything on this planet has a purpose ,so I place the annealed copper on the found object . I now reach for my..........
hammer . I proceed to inflect some pain on the metal .

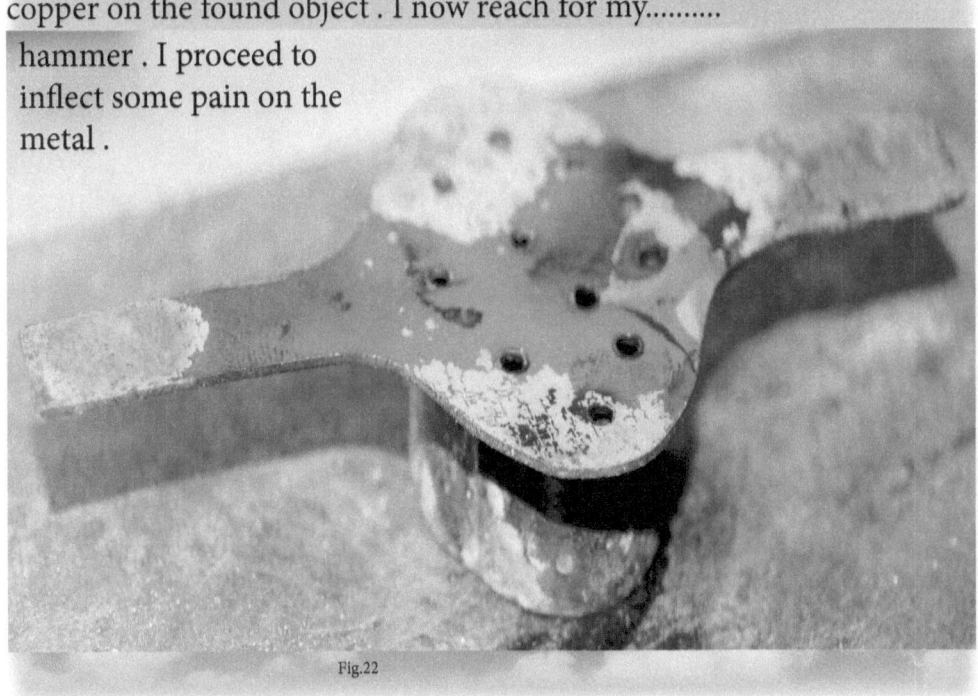

Fig.22

I apply the hammer to the soft copper and the contact produces
a sinking of the metal leaving us with this stage ....

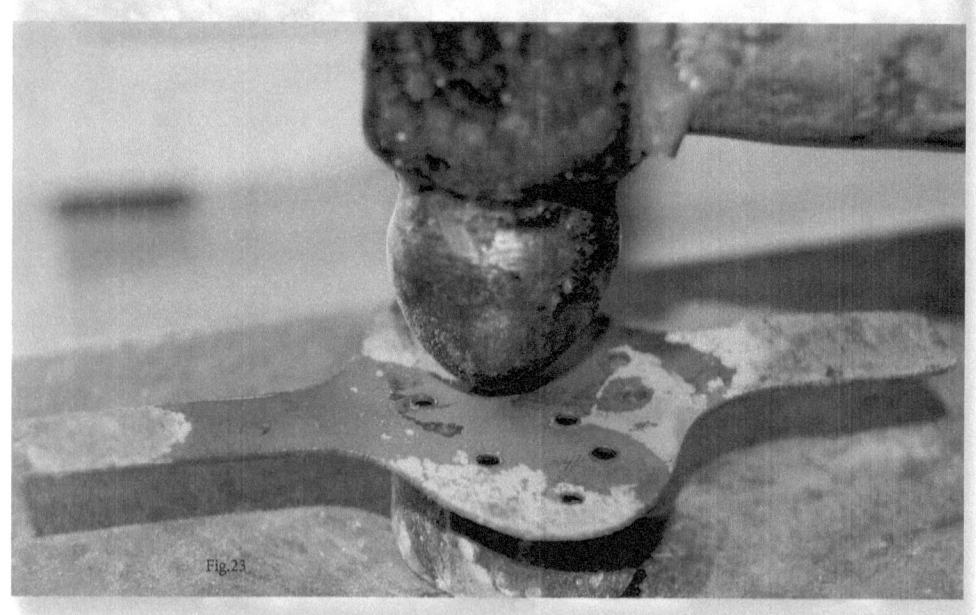

Fig.23

on the flip side .

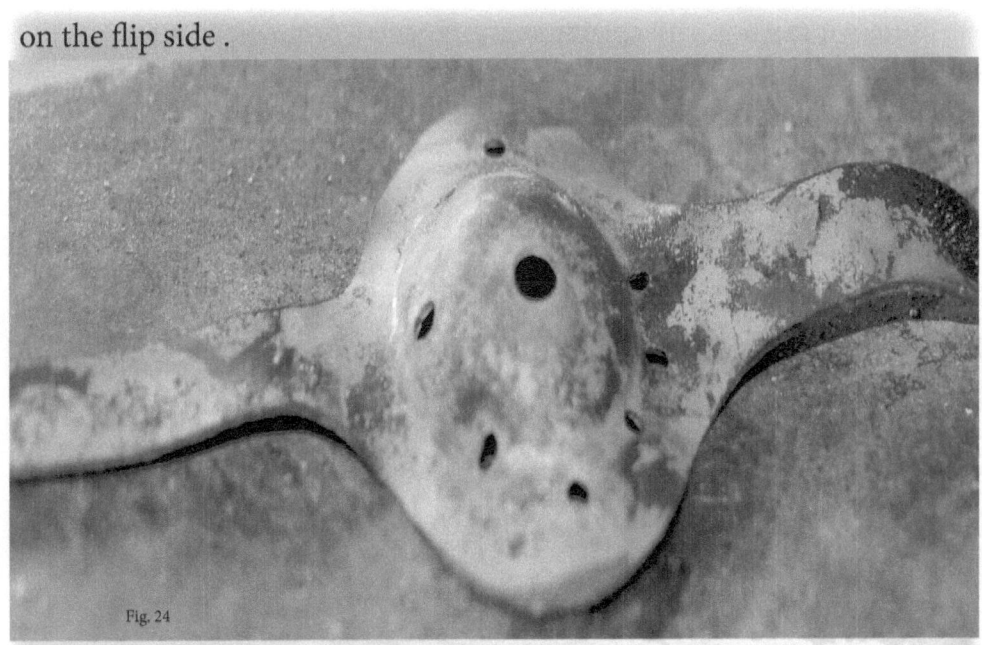

Fig. 24

Remember we have to clean off the fire-scale so I put the rings into a solution of pickle to get rid of the fire-scale.

This here is my homemade ring mandrel ,made from a broom
handle that had seen the end of his days or so he thought.
I told you that I make what I see no need to buy . If you are going
to create, then create.

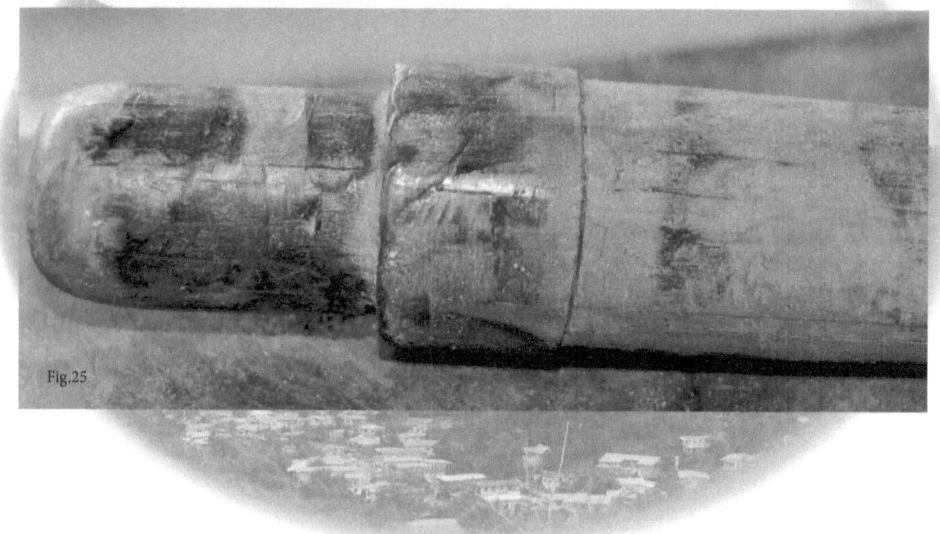

Fig.25

At this stage the copper is soft enough to bend around the mandrel with your hands ,but I will also use the......
hammer to tap it into shape .

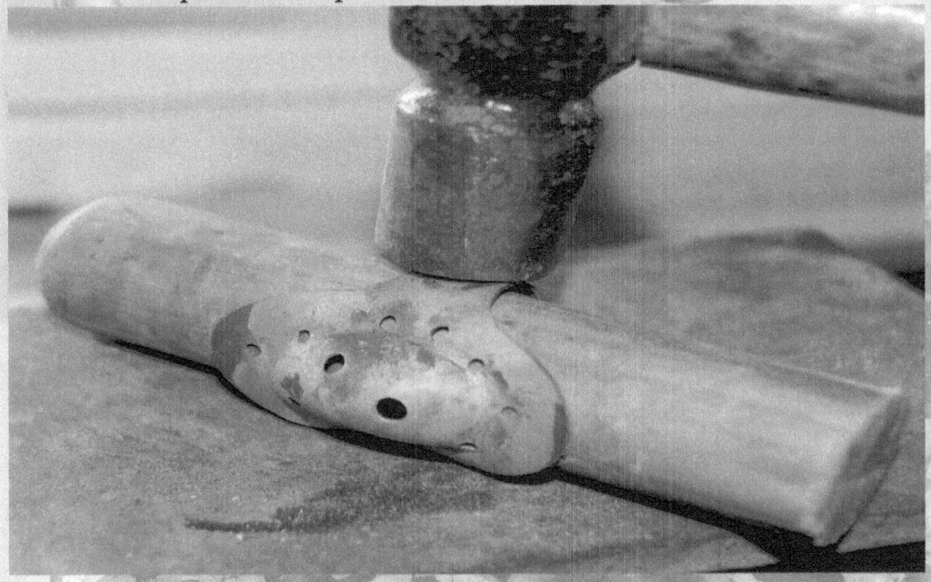

Fig.26

Inside of a crock pot from ... you guessed it .....a thrift store.
Here we have four rings pickled clean and also soldered. I
showed you the torch with which I soldered the rings.

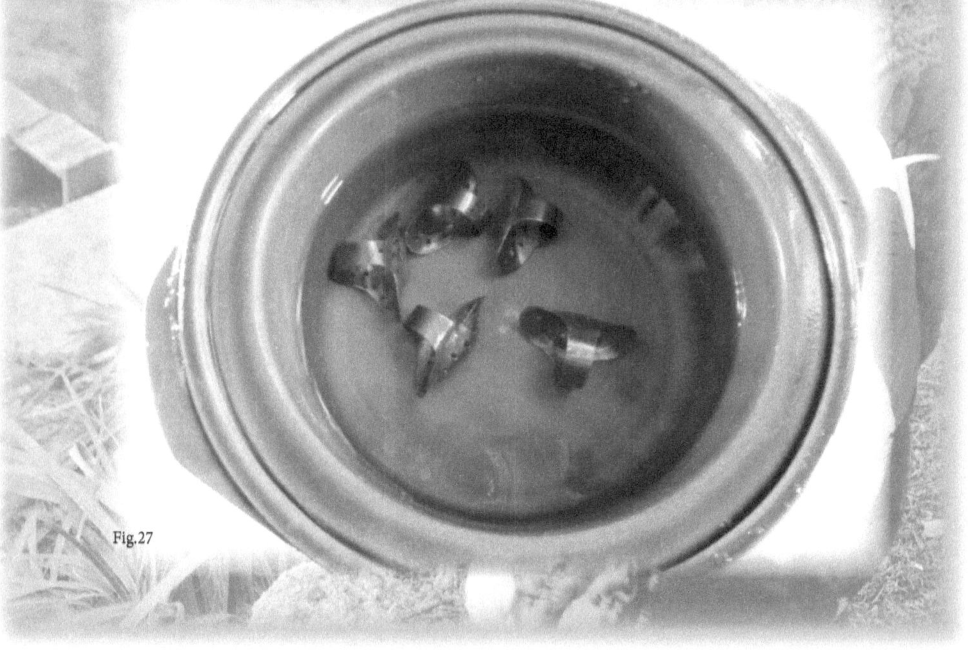

Fig.27

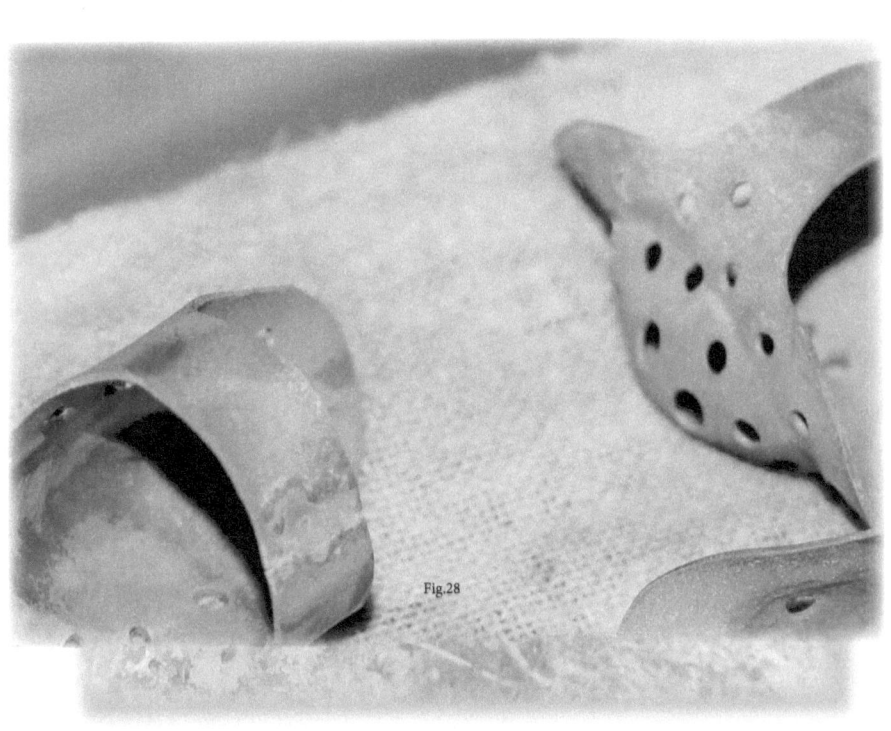

Fig.28

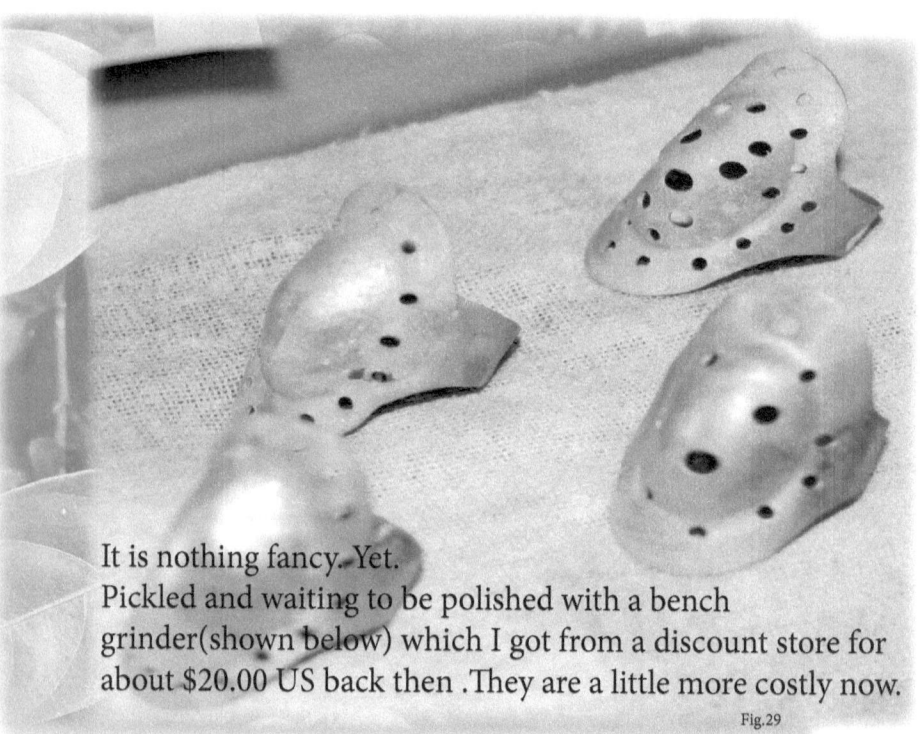

It is nothing fancy. Yet.
Pickled and waiting to be polished with a bench
grinder(shown below) which I got from a discount store for
about $20.00 US back then .They are a little more costly now.

Fig.29

We will now begin the polishing process. The finish line in in sight.

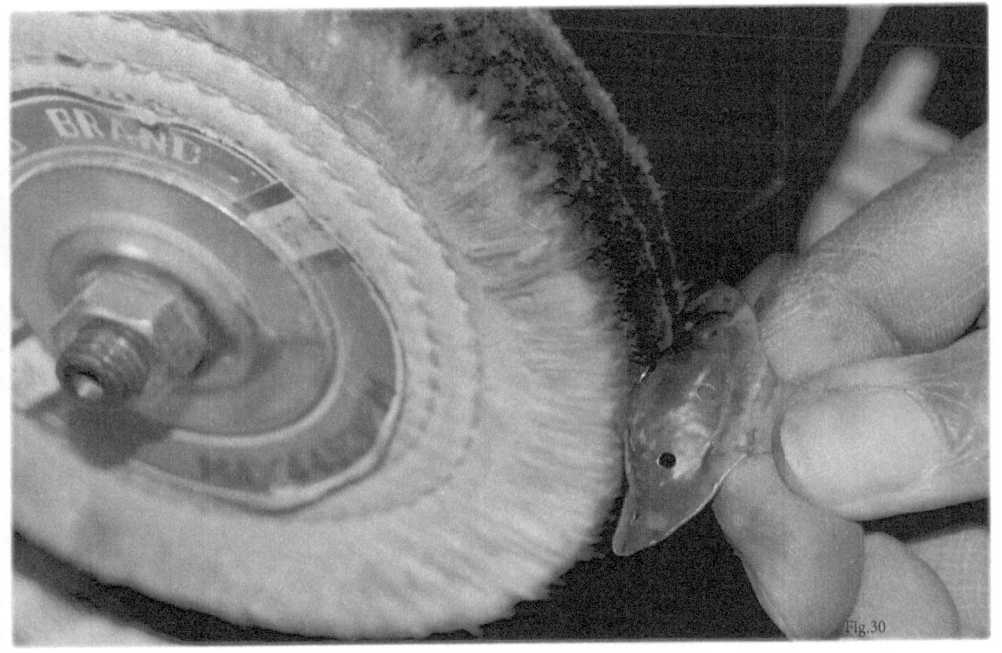

Fig.30

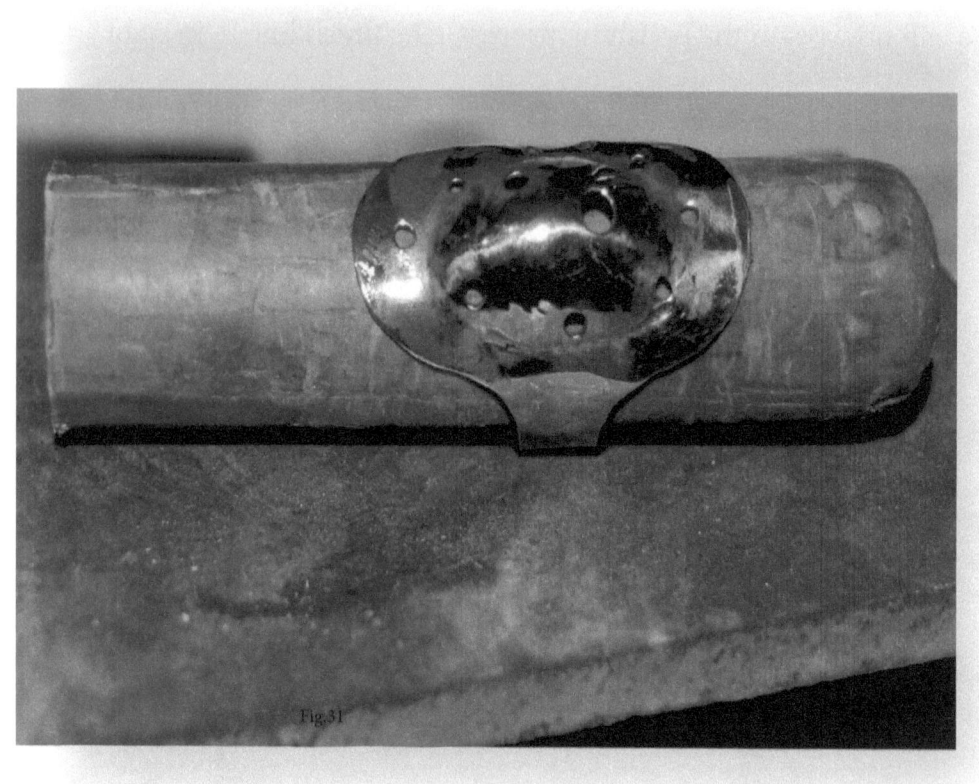

Fig. 31

Time to shine . We now have to clean off the rest of the fire scale that might have been too stubborn to come   loose in the pickle. Time to shine some more. And some more.

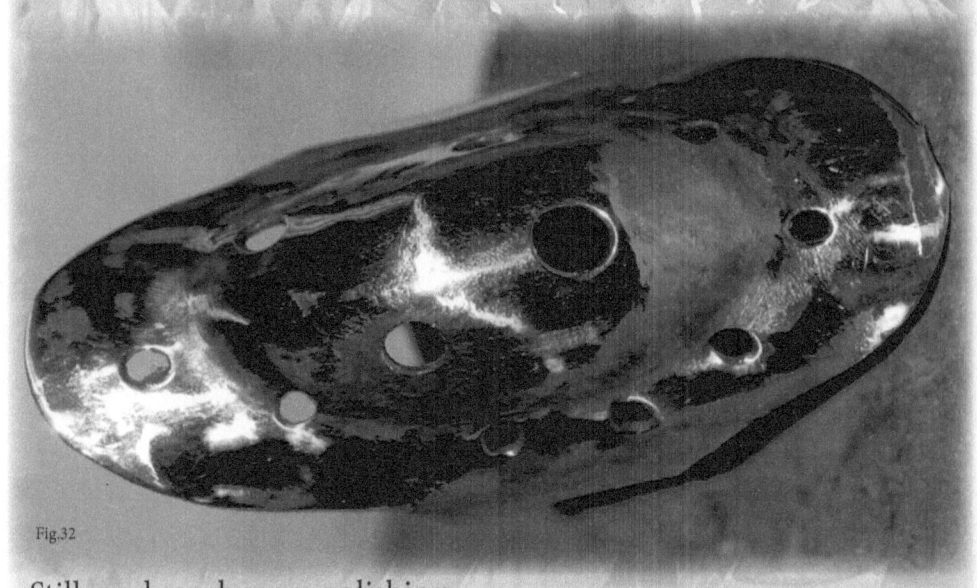

Fig.32

Still need much more polishing.

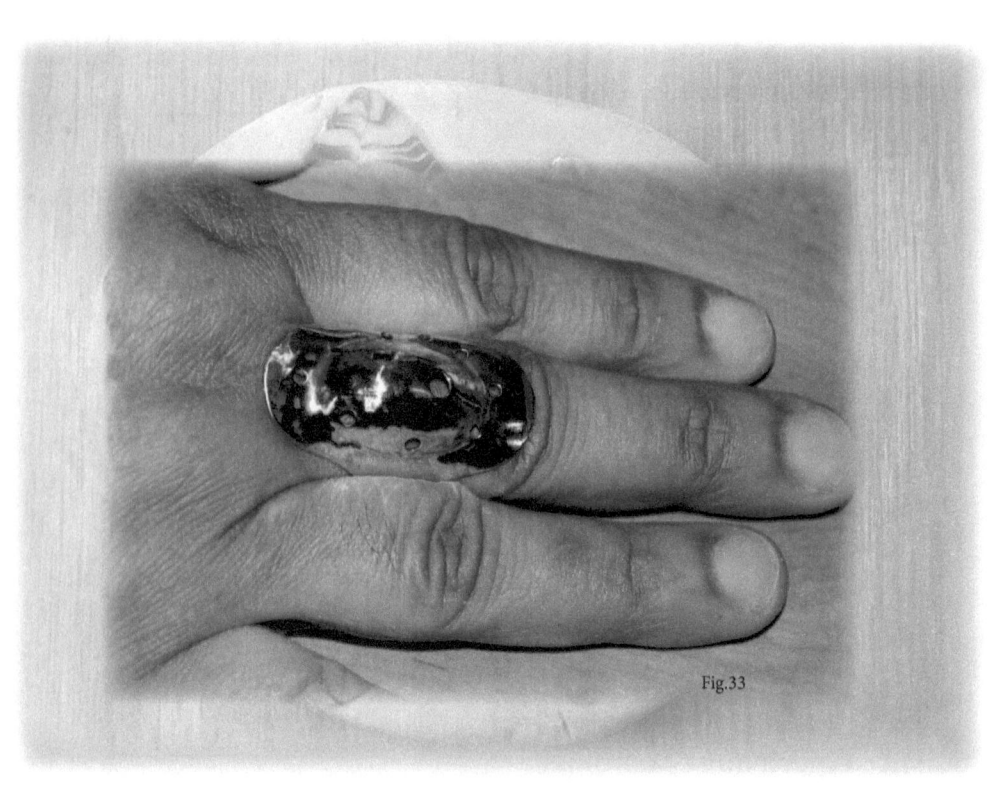

Fig.33

THE RESULT

And there it is people . After much labor we have emerged with objects of beauty. Go enhance the world with more wonderful things. Women go forward and flaunt !

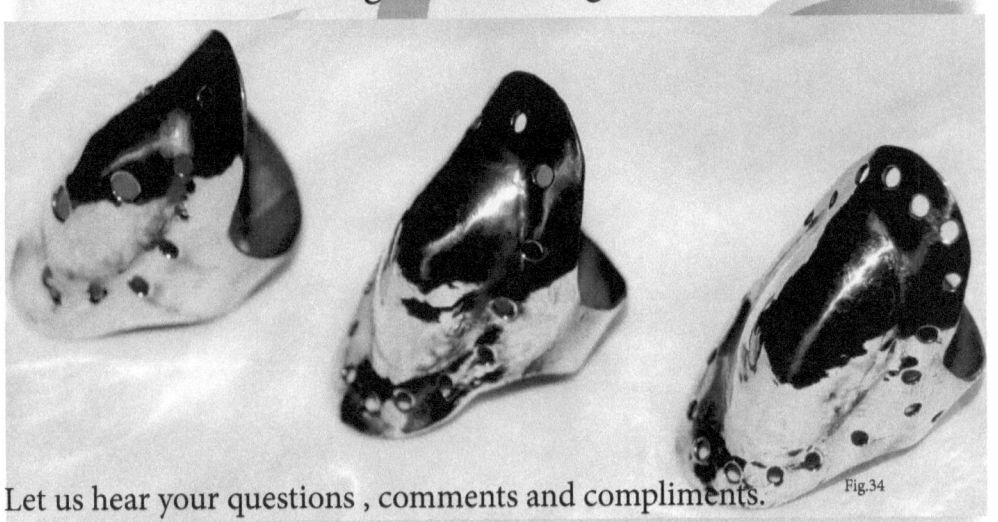

Let us hear your questions , comments and compliments.

Fig.34

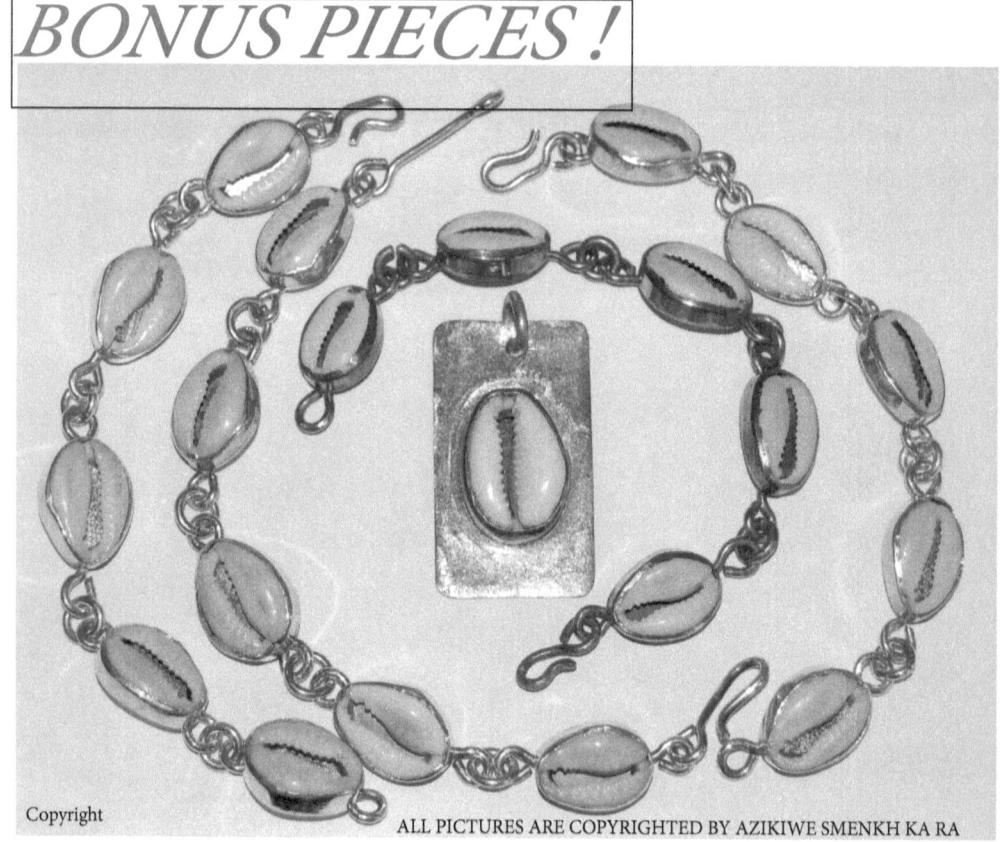

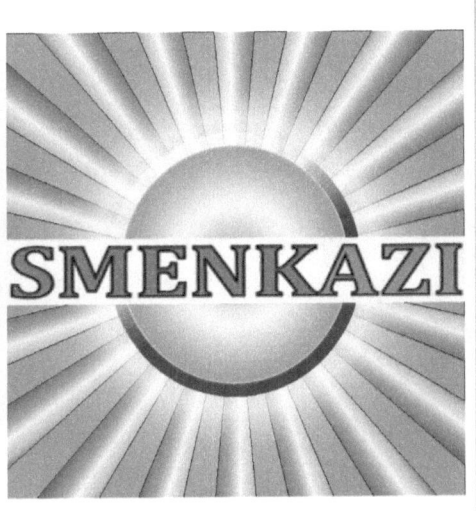

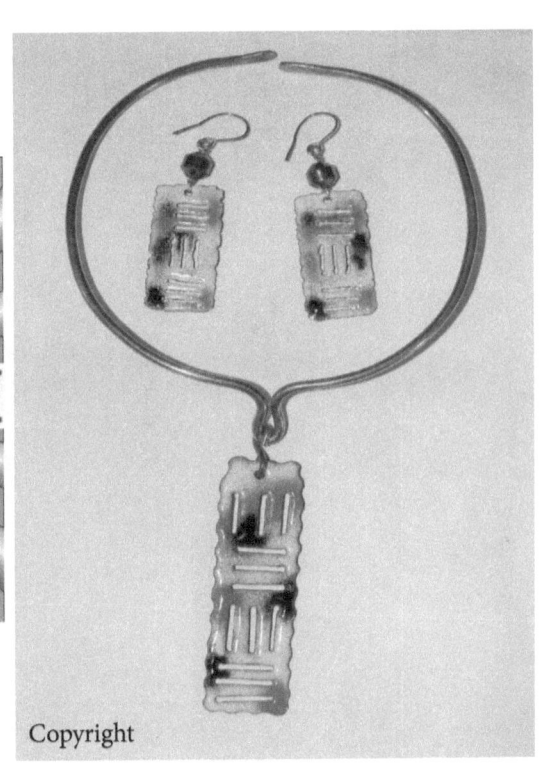

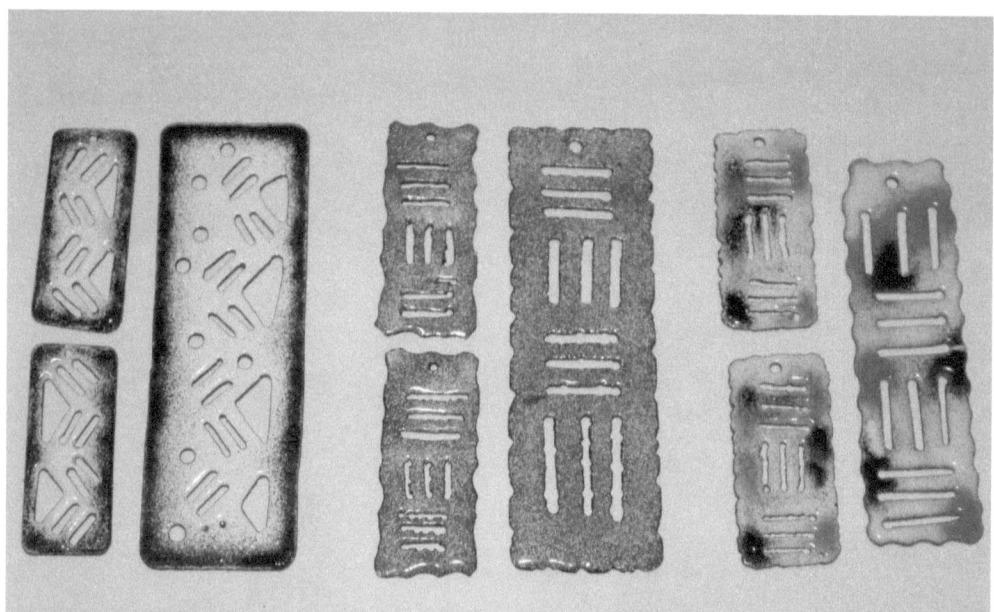

s m e n k a z i @ y a h o o . c o m